Winning

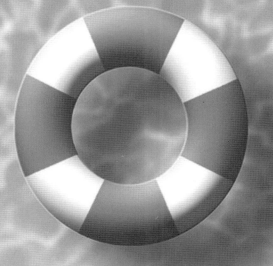

George B. Thompson

Abridged and adapted from the classic

Soul Winning

... because the night is coming

George Thompson

Table of Contents

Foreword
Chapter One – The Value of a Soul
Chapter Two – The Price of Soul Winning
Chapter Three – The Curse of Unconcern
Chapter Four – Won by One
Chapter Five – The Personal Touch
Chapter Six – Too Late!

Copyright © 2022 by
John Howard
All rights reserved

Foreword –

Some years ago, at Northwestern University in Illinois, twelve miles north of Chicago, a volunteer life-saving crew was formed that became famous for their efficient service. One morning, word came that a boat was in trouble on the lake. The students hurried to the shore, where they saw the "Lady Elgin" breaking in pieces. The passengers were in imminent danger.

Among the life-saving crew were two brothers from Iowa. One of the brothers stripped off all excess clothing, swam out, and brought a passenger to shore. He went again and brought another, then another, and another. He did this over and over until there were eight or nine on the shore of Lake Michigan that he had rescued. Chilled with cold, he stood trembling before the fire on the shore, but as he looked out into the lake, he saw another man in danger and said, "I must go again." Those around him urged, "If you go back out, it won't mean rescue for him, but death for you." Nevertheless, he broke from the crowd and plunged once more into the icy waters and brought a tenth, an eleventh, and a twelfth to the shore.

Again he stood by the fire, his strength apparently gone. As the crowd looked at him, so blue and chilled with cold, it seemed as if death had put its icy hand on him. But he looked again toward the wreck and saw others in peril. Once more, he struck out through the storm and brought the thirteenth, fourteenth, and fifteenth to the shore.

Cold and exhausted, he stood once more by the fire, but he could not rest. The victims of the storm lay heavy on his heart. Again he looked out and saw a drifting beam carrying a woman. As her husband struggled to save her, the beam drifted towards danger. Weak and exhausted, he again plunged into the water and brought the man and his wife safely to land.

That afternoon, as he lay in his bed, pale and exhausted, he asked, "Did I do my best? I am afraid I did not do my very best!" All night he tossed and turned, with his brother sitting beside his bed trying to comfort him, but he could only think about those who died. His brother said, "You saved seventeen!" He merely replied, "Oh, if only I could have saved one more!"

This incident expresses the purpose of this book. There is nothing new in these pages. A number of illustrations have been gathered from various sources, hoping to kindle a desire to save those being drawn down by the undertow of sin. If some are inspired with a stronger passion to rescue perishing souls from the fires of hell, then this book will have served its purpose. G.T.B.

Chapter One – The Value of a Soul

Many years ago, as a ship crossing the Pacific Ocean neared the shore, it struck a large jagged rock sticking out from one of the islands offshore. The powerful waves were quickly breaking the ship into pieces. Confusion was everywhere as the men and women aboard anxiously tried to find some way to escape their imminent death.

Among the passengers was a gold miner returning with his fortune from the rich goldfields of Australia. It was not too far to shore, and as he calculated his strength, he concluded that he was able to swim to land with his gold, representing his life work, buckled around his waist.

As he was just about to plunge into the foam-capped billows, a little girl came to him, and looking up in her helplessness, said beseechingly, "Will you please save me? I have no papa here to help me. Won't you, please?"

What should he do? To save this beautiful child, he must abandon the gold he had worked so long and hard for. He could not save both. The fury of the storm was quickly tearing the ship to pieces, and he had to decide quickly. He glanced at his gold, but the soft pressure of the child's hand and her pleading voice touched his heart.

The decision was made. Unbuckling the gold, he threw it on deck. Then fastening the child to him the best he could, he plunged into the angry sea. When he reached the land, he fell exhausted and unconscious.

When consciousness finally returned, he opened his eyes to see the child he had saved standing by his side, with tears of joy and love flooding down her cheeks. The ship had disappeared, and with it, the gold he had worked so hard for. But he had saved a human life.

Certainly, we would all agree that the miner made a wise and noble decision, but we should take to heart an important lesson from this. A world is doomed to eternal death, sinking beneath the curse of sin. All around us are lost souls who are silently longing for salvation. These should be more precious to us than all the money in the world.

A young man, distinguished for his attainments in mathematics, challenged his fellow students to try and stump him with difficult problems. One day, a classmate came to his study and handed him a folded paper. Looking at him, he said, "Here is a problem I want you to solve for me," and then he immediately left the room. The young math major quickly unfolded the paper and read the words, "For what will it profit a man if he gains the whole world, and loses his own soul? Or what will a man give in exchange for his soul?" The question soon led to the young man's conversion. Certainly, this is the most important subject that the human mind has ever contemplated.

All around us, every day, men are playing with their souls as if they were toys. They need to see how valuable their soul is and what it will be worth to be saved, to dwell among the supernal glories of the new earth, to fly through the eternal home of the Creator. But blinded by sin, many people are selling their souls for the cheap, temporary pleasures of this life.

It has been said that visitors to the Niagara Falls were at once directed to a spot on the edge of a cliff where a thoughtless young lady lost her life. Enraptured with the beauty of the scene before her and wanting to pick a flower from a cliff where no human had ever gone, she looked over the edge and caught sight of a beautiful flower. In her excitement, she leaned over the brink of the yawning chasm and reached out her arm in an attempt to grasp the flower. But suddenly, the earth beneath her gave way, and with a shriek, she fell into the foaming waters where she was swept away. Tragically, she sacrificed her life for a fading flower.

As foolish as this seems, many of us are doing the same thing and worse. The majority of people in the world are sacrificing their souls for the fading things of this life! While reaching for the riches, fame, and pleasures of earth, life ends, and all is lost.

It is horrible to see a field of grain blasted and swept away by a violent tornado. It is even worse to see fires and floods destroy some beautiful city, with its homes and inhabitants. But it is infinitely sadder to see sin ruin a soul for whom Jesus died.

Imagine you see a man drowning in the distance. As his strength is waning and he is about to go under for the last time, you dive in and rescue him. As a result, he lives twenty years longer—a loving husband and a happy father. You added twenty years to his existence. But one soul saved in the kingdom of God will live in the beauty and bliss of heaven long enough to equal the total ages of everyone who has ever lived, from creation to the end of time, and even then, eternity will have only begun. With no more curse of sin in the world, all eternity will stretch out before them to bask in the sunshine of God's presence through countless ages.

Think of the unending ages of bliss that await the saved! To even give temporary joy to someone depressed or suffering in this life is a worthy act, but to see a lost soul turn to Christ and gain the bliss of eternity in heaven as a result of our labors will be beyond anything we can imagine. There is no greater joy than to see lost souls receive eternal life.

Here, men long for the things they can never attain, but there, every need will be supplied as we bask in the sunlight of God's presence. Here, joy and pleasure fade away, leaving an aching void in our hearts, but there, at God's right hand, will be "fullness of joy" and "pleasures forevermore" (Ps. 16:11). Here, people grow old and die, but there, there will be "no more death, nor sorrow, nor crying" (Rev. 21:4). In heaven, all tears will be wiped from our eyes. Peace will flow like a river through our souls. Light and joy will spring forth from our hearts. All this and infinitely more is within the reach of every sinner, but now is the time to rescue those who are still lost.

Now is the time to search for lost souls who are searching and longing for more than this life has to offer. As we enjoy the bliss of eternity together, those people we have played a part in saving will be forever grateful to us. With immortal vision, we must look at the perishing world around us and determine to work harder than ever before. All eternity waits before us, and while it is day, the work must go on.

Chapter Two – The Price of Soul Winning

"Hiking through the woods, two men were overtaken in a terrible blizzard one cold, wintry day, out west. Eventually, the dreadful truth started to sink in that they were lost and freezing to death. One of the men finally said to the other, 'I can't go any farther. I have to sit down. You go on. Tell my wife and family what happened.' Hearing these words, his friend became aroused, refusing to leave him. He pushed him. He urged him to struggle on and cling to hope. When his friend could not walk any farther, he lifted him on his shoulders and carried him in a desperate search for shelter. Finally, a cabin was located where they were greeted by the protection and comfort of a warm home. Upon contemplation, it dawned on the man that his efforts to save his friend ended up saving himself.

"Recently, research conducted among the ruins of Pompeii, which was destroyed by a volcano, turned up an amazing find which told its own story. It was the body of a crippled boy. His foot was lame, and around his body was the beautiful, bejeweled arm of a woman. The find told a very simple story. The great stream of fire had rushed down from the volcano. As the crowd was fleeing for their lives, this crippled boy was unable to move fast enough. The woman's heart was touched, and as she threw her arm around the boy to aid his escape, they were overtaken by the flood of lava, and both lost their lives. The arm that was stretched out to save another was the only part of the woman that remained. All the rest of the brave rescuer's body had gone. The saving part was saved. Only that mercifully outstretched arm to save another was itself saved" (Gordon, Samuel, *Quiet Talks with World Winners*, Updated, pp. 117, 118).

It is equally true that those who lose their life for Christ's sake will find it. Those who, in their eagerness to save others, give themselves up unselfishly to this work will find that they have saved their own souls from becoming cold and barren, and instead, have received a life filled with the richness and joy of heaven.

"People said Harriet Newell's beautiful life was wasted when she gave it to missionary work, only to die in her first year of service, before she even got to tell one unbeliever the story of Jesus. But was that lovely young life really wasted? Not at all! After her death, her diary was published, and she became one of the greatest inspirations for missionary work. Her influence spread everywhere, inspiring thousands of men and women to service by the story of her consecration. Harriet Newell could have never done the work in her home that she did in that one short year of service, by giving her life to what seemed like a useless sacrifice. She lost her life that she might save it. She died that she might live. She offered herself as a living sacrifice that she might become useful.

"We must all do the same if we wish to ever be a real blessing in the world. We must be willing to lose our life, to sacrifice ourselves, to give up our own way, our own ease, our own comfort, and possibly even our own life. On occasions, there come times when one's life must literally be lost in order to be saved."

"One afternoon in an England mine, there was a fearful explosion. Immediately, men came rushing up from the lower level, right into the area of the deadly after-blast. Seeing the danger, one man stood there in the shaft, warning the men to go in the other direction. When some urged him to go find safety as well, he replied, 'No, someone has to stay here and guide the others out.' The man was willing to lay down his life for his co-workers. Can we find any greater heroism in this world than that?

"During the Civil War, there was a bloody battle at Fredericksburg, Virginia. As the relentless gunfire continued, hundreds of Union soldiers lay wounded on the field. Throughout the night and all through the next day, the place was swept by artillery fire from both sides. No one dared to venture onto the field to relieve the sufferers, but they were haunted by the perpetual moans. Agonizing cries for water echoed across the field, but there was no response except the roar of the guns. Finally, one brave Southern soldier behind the ramparts decided he could no longer endure the pitiful cries, and his compassion for the wounded grew greater than his love of life itself.

"'General, I can't stand this,' Richard Kirkland called out to his commander. 'These poor men out there have been praying for water all night and all day. I can't take it anymore. May I please have permission to carry water to them?'

"The general assured him that he would be instantly killed if he went out on that field, but he begged so earnestly that the officer, admiring his noble devotion to humanity, could not refuse his request. Provided with a supply of water, the brave soldier stepped over the wall and went on his Christ-like errand. From both sides, wondering eyes looked on as he knelt by the nearest sufferer, gently raised his head, and held the cooling cup to his parched lips. At once, the Union soldiers understood what the soldier in gray was doing for their wounded comrades, and not a shot was fired. For an hour and a half, he continued his work of mercy, giving drink to the thirsty, straightening cramped and mangled limbs, pillowing men's heads on their knapsacks, and spreading blankets and army coats over them as tenderly as a mother would cover her child; and the whole time, not one gun was fired until this angel ministry was finished.

"We have to admire the heroism that led this brave soldier to utterly forget himself, even risking his own life, all for the sake of showing mercy to his enemies. There is more dignity in five minutes of self-renunciation than in a whole lifetime of self-interest and self-seeking. There is something Christ-like in it. Our greatest selfish strivings appear poor, small, and insignificant beside such noble deeds.

"We must adopt the same spirit if we wish to become a blessing to the world, in any sense of the word. We must die to live. We must lose our life to save it. We must lay self on the altar to be consumed in the fire of love in order to glorify God and do good to men. It is only when self is sacrificed, burned on the altar of consecration, and consumed in the hot flames of love, that our work becomes our best, a fit offering to be made to our King.

"We must not be afraid of losing ourselves in sacrifice, renunciation, and self-annihilation. God will remember every act of love, every time we were willing to forget our needs, and every time we were willing to empty our lives for the service of others. Even though we may work in obscure places where no human tongue will ever give us praise, there is a record kept in heaven, and one day a glorious reward will be given. Isn't God's praise better than man's?...

"Mary's ointment was apparently wasted when she broke the vase and poured it on her Lord's feet, but what if she left the ointment in the unbroken vase? Would anyone remember the ointment? Would there be any mention of it on the pages of the gospel? Would her generous act be told all over the world? She broke the vase and poured it out. She sacrificed it. She lost it, and now that spilled jar of perfume fills the whole earth. We may keep our life if we want. We may carefully preserve it, spending it on worldly pleasures, but we will have no reward in the end. Only if we empty it out in loving service will we make it a lasting blessing to the world which will be remembered forever" (Miller, J.R., *Making the Most of Life*," Updated, pp. 5-11).

Chapter Three – The Curse of Unconcern

So many Christians today are resting at ease in the midst of a perishing world. This explains why there are so few converts in our churches today, why there is so little burden for souls, so few tears shed, and so little effort put forth for the conversion of sinners. A group of Christians once asked the famous evangelist Dwight L. Moody how to become a soul-winner. He replied, "Get to work." That is the only way to win souls. We must give ourselves to days of labor and nights of prayer. It is startling that so many Christians who claim to believe that Jesus is coming soon and that the judgments of God are about to fall on a lost world are so indifferent to the eternal future of their neighbors, friends, and relatives.

In secular matters, we often express great concern. When the bank crashes where someone's savings were deposited, we show great concern! If we see a friend in danger, we will exert tireless efforts to save his life. But for those in danger of eternal damnation, we often show little or no concern. Rowland Hill, whose heart burned with a passion for the lost, was often called crazy because of this burden. In response, he related an event, saying, "While I walked down the road, I saw a gravel pit cave in

16

and bury three men alive. I quickly ran to the rescue and shouted for help until the people heard me in the town almost a mile away. Nobody called me crazy then. But when I see sinners sinking into the pit of eternal death and cry out, hoping they will see their danger and escape, the people say I have gone crazy. Well, maybe I have, but I wish all of God's children would be fired up with the same crazy desire to save the lost!"

Professed Christians work hard for money, but neglect souls whose value is beyond estimate. A writer once put it this way. He said, "Suppose someone was to offer me ten thousand dollars for every soul that I earnestly try to lead to Christ. Would I work harder to lead more souls to him than I am doing right now? Is it possible that I would attempt to do more for money, even at the risk of blunders or ridicule, than what I hesitate or shrink from doing now in obedience to God's command? Is my love of money stronger than my love of God, or of souls?" The same writer takes the question a step farther, adding, "Suppose I saw a blind man unknowingly approaching the edge of a high cliff. Imagine that I sat by without concern, or without making any effort to warn him, or save him from certain death. Wouldn't I be as guilty of his death in God's sight then I would be if I had murdered

17

him? The death of a life that could have been prevented is a terrible thing, but what about the preventable death of a human soul, or many souls?"

"Christ gave his own life to save souls, and yet you who have known His love make so little effort to impart the blessings of His grace to those for whom He died. Such indifference and neglect of duty is an amazement to the angels. In the judgment you must meet the souls you have neglected. In that great day you will be self-convicted" (White, E.G., *Testimonies for the Church, Vol. 6,* p. 425). Meeting the souls in the judgment who were lost because of our unconcern and lack of effort will be an awful experience. We need to go through Gethsemane so that the chill of indifference can be taken from our hearts and that we may be warmed with a newfound zeal for service.

"All can do something in the work. None will be pronounced guiltless before God, unless they have worked earnestly and unselfishly for the salvation of souls" (White, E.G., *Testimonies for the Church,*" Vol. 5, p. 395).

"How would a father and mother feel, did they know that their child, lost in the cold and the snow, had been passed by, and left to perish, by those who might have saved it? Would they not be terribly grieved, wildly indignant? Would they not denounce those murderers with wrath hot as their tears, intense as their love? The sufferings of every man are the sufferings of God's child, and those who reach out no helping hand to their perishing fellow beings provoke His righteous anger" (White, E.G., *The Desire of Ages*, p. 825).

"Many, many are approaching the day of God doing nothing, shunning responsibilities, and as the result they are religious dwarfs. So far as work for God is concerned, the pages of their life history present a mournful blank... In the day of God how many will confront us and say, 'I am lost! I am lost! and you never warned me; you never entreated me to come to Jesus. Had I believed as you did, I would have followed every judgment-bound soul with prayers and tears and warnings'" (White, E.G., *The Review and Herald*, May 22, 1888).

Why not decide to become an intercessory Christian for the unsaved? Why not decide to shake off the ice of frozen indifference, and become a soul-winner for life? And why not begin now? Where should you begin? Start with the person next to you, and don't let your apparent lack of qualification stand in the way. A poor, stammering Christian, his heart consumed with a love for souls, can do more than the most eloquent speaker who has no burden for the lost.

We should work while it is day, because the night is quickly coming when no man can work.

"In a town in New England a well was being dug. When the work was nearly finished, while one man was still at the bottom, the earth caved in and buried him. Instantly the alarm was sent out, and mechanics, farmers, merchants, lawyers, hurried breathlessly to the rescue. Ropes, ladders, spades, and shovels were brought by eager, willing hands. 'Save him, O save him!' was the cry.

"Men worked with desperate energy, till the sweat stood in beads upon their brows and their arms trembled with the exertion. At length a pipe was thrust down, through which they shouted to the man to answer if he were still alive. The response came, 'Alive, but make haste. It is fearful in here.' With a shout of joy they renewed their efforts, and at last he was reached and saved, and the cheer that went up seemed to pierce the very heavens. 'He is saved!' echoed through every street in the town.

"Was this too great zeal and interest, too great enthusiasm, to save one man? It surely was not; but what is the loss of temporal life in comparison with the loss of a soul? If the threatened loss of a life will arouse in human hearts a feeling so intense, should not the loss of a soul arouse even deeper solicitude in men who claim to realize the danger of those apart from Christ? Shall not the servants of God show as great zeal in laboring for the salvation of souls as was shown for the life of that one man buried in a well?" (White, E.G., *Christian Service*, p. 94).

All around us are multitudes of lost souls who are spiritually blind. Some of them are being led blindly by others who have no spiritual eyesight. Within our reach are those who unknowingly are making their way toward the cliff of eternal death. Their feet are even now standing on the verge of the cliff. One more step and they will go over, disappearing into the dark cavern of eternity below from which there is no return. Some of these are our neighbors, or friends, or possibly even our own family members. Look at these souls as they march on their way to perdition! There they go, marching on to destruction and death! We can save some of them if we will simply make the effort, and yet many are sitting in cold, silent indifference, making no effort to warn them of the danger which lies just ahead, almost in sight. Can we do this and still talk about our hope of heaven? Are we showing them sympathy because they do not have the light we have? A stationary lighthouse is fine, but it cannot take the place of a human rescue team. Life-savers are desperately needed.

Chapter Four – Won by One

Navy rescue teams do not save shipwrecked people in groups. They save them one at a time. A man getting ready to sink beneath the waves for the last time is rescued. When all hope is gone, a boy about to drown is reached just in time and brought safely back into the lifeboat. A sailor clings to the rigging as the vessel is quickly breaking to pieces, but by heroic effort, he is saved too. And the work goes on. The faithful, life-saving rescuers proceed to save people one at a time until everyone is safe.

In the distance, a building is on fire. The violent flames are eating their way through the partitions into every room. On the upper floors, there are people in danger, but the only way to rescue them is from outside, so the firemen climb the ladders over and over again, pulling people from the doomed building one at a time until everyone is safe.

A sailing ship was driven towards the rocky coast of Scotland by a violent hurricane. The wind and waves were quickly tearing the ship to pieces against the rocks offshore when a group of locals caught word of the vessel's plight and went to the rescue. The storm shrieked like a band of demons bent on an errand of destruction, but in spite of the danger and possible loss to their own men, the rescue team sent a boat out, making heroic efforts to save the crew. After completing the mission, they started back to the shore, but as they drew away from the vessel, someone spotted a man who had been overlooked, still clinging to the rigging of the doomed ship. His face was shaded with a look of despair, but the men on the ship said, "We can't go back to get him. The waves are too strong. If we try, our boat will be dashed to pieces on the rocks, and we will all die." So they left the man still clinging to the rigging and headed for the shore.

When they landed, one of the young men called out, "Someone come with me. Let's go get that man stuck on the ship." His mother, now standing at his side, threw her arms around him and pleaded, "Please don't go. Your father was a sailor and was lost at sea in a storm just like this many years ago, and eight years ago, your brother William went to sea, and no one has heard from him since. No doubt he also died at sea. If you go and die, what will I do? I am poor and old. You are my only support. You must not go."

Gently removing her arms from around him, he said, "I'm sorry, Mother, but there is a man about to die out there. The ship is about to sink, and I've got to try and save him if I can. If I die doing my duty, God will take care of you." Then, kissing her pale, wrinkled face sweetly on the cheek, he and his companion returned to the boat and headed back into the storm.

Everyone on the shore anxiously waited for what seemed like hours, staring out into the storm, hoping for the boat's safe return. Finally, through the mist and gathering darkness, they saw something in the distance making its way back towards the shore. Weary and disheveled, the two brave men struggled with their remaining strength to reach land. When they came close to the shore, some of the men called out, "Did you save the man on the ship?" Lifting his hands to his mouth to trumpet the words, the young man called back, "Yes. And tell my mother I've found my brother William." It was the only man he saved, but the one he pulled from the rigging of the sinking ship was his long-lost brother.

The same may be said of us. All around us there are souls perishing. All around us are men and women clinging to some earthly treasure that will soon sweep them away by the coming storm. They are our lost brothers and sisters, and it is our duty to rescue them, even if it is at the cost of our own comfort or even our earthly life itself. Thousands are adrift, ready to be sucked under the fearful undertow of sin. God desires to work through us to save as many people as possible, but He needs workers. He is depending on you and me. Saved souls must be picked up carefully, lovingly, one day at a time. We must "hunt them from every mountain, and from every hill, and out of the holes of the rocks."

It was once said that "it is not enough to pray for the conversion of sinners; it is not enough to look with fear upon the palaces of the rich, or with solicitude upon the hovels of the poor. Our feet must cross their threshold." If we will only search, we will gradually find one here and another there, but we must be consistent in our search. We must fix our eyes on the stormy seas of life around us, watching for those lost souls who are clinging to the rigging, looking for a hand to reach out and save them.

The aggressive principle in soul-winning has been appropriately illustrated in the following story. Vicksburg, Mississippi, was a key location in winning the Civil War, and the war was heating up. "It seems that face to face with Vicksburg, the Eleventh Indiana military unit was badly cut up, so they sent home for reserves. New soldiers arrived, but most of them knew nothing about fighting. They had never been in a battle, and they were to enter a hard one at their very first fight. Among the new reserves was a gaunt, tall Hoosier, who the men simply called Peter Apples. Peter had never fought. All that he knew about soldiering was that a soldier was supposed to do whatever he was told. So when his commander said, 'Forward March, double-quick,' why, Peter double-quicked! There was nothing else to do.

"In the heat of the battle, the tall thin soldier marched forward. While the rest kept pace with him for a while, the fire of the enemy was so hot that many of the rookie soldiers became frightened and fell back. But Peter was running so fast that he couldn't stop. He just kept moving straight ahead until he finally ran up on the enemy's rampart. As one of the enemy soldiers charged him, Peter clipped him on the head, took him by the back of the neck, turned him around, and started carrying him back to his camp. Some other soldiers spotted him, but they did not dare shoot for fear they would kill their own man, so Peter kept on running back to his home base. When he finally came panting back to his own camp, dragging the enemy soldier, his men rallied around him and asked, 'Peter, where did you get him?' Pointing behind him towards the enemy's rampart, Peter replied, 'Why, I got him up there! There are lots of them up there. Every one of you could've had one if you had only gone after him.'

"As we look out and see the flood of humanity in our great cities and across the plains of our land, men and women being swept down in the awful torrent of eternal death, we hear that cry ringing in our ears, 'There are lots of them there, and every one of you can have one if you will just go after him.' And that's just what Jesus said to us. 'Go ye.'"

The trouble with so many of us is simply that we do not go after souls as we should. We wait for a convenient time or for some big event to gather in the masses when there are individuals all around us each day waiting to be rescued. The unnumbered millions around the throne will not have been rescued in groups, but one by one.

We cannot become disheartened because we are unable to stir the masses by some great speech or some powerful appeal. Just reach out to one soul. Almost anyone can be interested in a crowd, but it is an indication of true greatness to be interested in one soul. Start with the people nearest to you. Maybe someone in your own home or an unconverted neighbor. The prospect may not look encouraging, the material may seem unpromising, but take courage. Think of Jesus and Nicodemus, or of the Samaritan woman, and labor on, knowing that your work, if done faithfully, will one day be rewarded.

Chapter Five – The Personal Touch

Clay Trumbull, in his book, "*Individual Work for Individuals*," relates the sentiments of Joel Stratton towards John B. Gough, the man who led him to Christ, with the words, "My friend, it may be a small matter for you to speak the one word for Christ that wins a needy soul – a *small matter to you*, but it is *everything to him*.' It is forgetting this truth that causes personal work to be neglected."

A visitor at a pottery observed a workman molding a clay pot. The process seemed slow, and the visitor asked if there was any tool they could use to do the work faster. "No," replied the potter, "we have tried several, but somehow in this work, we must have the human touch." The same thing could be said of molding human souls for the Master's use. We need the personal touch.

A Christian worker passing by a crowd stopped to see what was going on. As he pressed through the crowd, he found, in the middle, a small child who had become separated from friends and didn't know his way home. The child looked up, and seeing the look of sympathy on the gentleman's face, the child stretched out his hands and pleaded, "Please show me my way home?" The man later said, "That cry has been sounding in my ears ever since, every time I see a wandering soul like that boy in the city."

Within the reach of all, there are many lost souls who need someone to show them the way home. Their condition itself is a silent appeal to us for help. It may be someone who works in the office with you, the girl ringing up your items at the grocery store, or the person delivering your mail. It may be your neighbor, the woman up the road, or even someone you see at your church every week. It seems unspeakably sad to think that we see some of these people week after week with no personal effort being made to bring them to Christ. Why is that? Why do we often feel such indifference when so much is at stake?

If we could fully realize the value of even one soul, maybe it would help us become more active and earnest in the work of saving souls. It may help those who are parents to consider how much your own child is worth. What would you give to have them saved? I read about an incident that happened many years ago, even before the invention of cars, which impressed this thought on my mind.

"A farmer in North Carolina was driving two headstrong horses into the town. Stopping in front of one of the stores, he was about to enter, when his horses became spooked. He jumped up in front of them and heroically grabbed the reigns. Maddened by strange noises, the horses began running wildly down the street with the man still clinging to the bridles. They continued on until the horses, wild with frenzy, reared up on their hind legs and then came crashing down, falling right on the man. When the people came to rescue the bleeding body of the man and found him nearly dead, a friend bent over him tenderly and asked, 'Why did you sacrifice your life for horses and wagon?' He gasped and muttered with his last breath, 'Go look in the wagon.' They turned, and there, asleep in the straw, lay his little boy. As they laid the mangled form of the hero in his grave, no one said, 'The sacrifice was too great.'"

It was his little boy sleeping in the wagon that caused this father to sacrifice his life. He was not thinking about the value of the team of horses or the wagon, but about his boy. He was entirely oblivious to danger and willing, if necessary, to die to save his little boy sleeping in the straw. Was the sacrifice he made too great to rescue his child from death?

There are other boys all around us worth just as much as that boy. They play on the very streets around our home, sit in our church pews, and pass by us every day. Your boy may not be among them, but they are somebody's boys. Shouldn't we make the same tireless efforts to save their souls for eternity as the father who risked his life to save his boy from being killed? When we are willing to sacrifice and die so others can be saved, then we will really begin to see sinners come to Christ.

There is great power in being sociable and warm-hearted. We could accomplish so much if we would simply manifest a personal interest in others. Many people can be won this way. Our teaching and warnings should fall like gentle drops of rain, not like hail. I sometimes fear that many of our efforts are illustrated by the following near-fatal incident.

A man was drowning in a pond on a cold day. Seeing him, another grabbed a nearby board and held it out towards the drowning man, but the end of the plank was covered with ice. The man repeatedly tried to grab it and save himself, but he couldn't get hold of it. Finally, in despair, he cried out, "Give me the other end of the plank. This end is icy!" In our efforts to help others, we need to be sure that we are not holding out the icy end of the plank. We must be careful that our words are not chilled by the icy atmosphere of indifference, carelessness, or coldness.

As the overshadowing cloud of the world's doom grows darker, God's people should be inspired with greater zeal than ever. We need to put forth untiring personal efforts to warn and save the souls of our neighbors, friends, and family. If we saw them in a burning building, in great danger of being consumed by the angry flames, we would put forth tireless efforts to save them from such an agonizing death. Nothing could get in our way from trying to rescue them, but a more terrible fate awaits those who are unconverted in our homes, down our streets, and throughout our neighborhoods. While many of us sit unmoved and indifferent, standing idly by, they are being swept over the great Niagara of eternal ruin. It is time for everyone who believes that Christ is coming back soon to earnestly begin missionary work for those around us. Our greatest need is a burden for souls. Many do far too little in soul-winning. Every unsaved, unwarned soul should pain our hearts.

While visiting a campground, the word went out that a little boy, who had been left in a tent while the parents were attending a morning meeting, was lost. Soon the whole camp was stirred. Tears were shed, and anxiety was seen on every face. Breakfast was forgotten. No one cared about eating at a time like this. Large groups of people scattered in every direction and continued searching until the lost boy was found, and yet all around us are lost boys and girls, and no anxiety is seen. Why is there such indifference in our hearts? We must pray for God to give us a passion for the lost.

If someone we dearly loved was facing a death sentence and we could receive a pardon from the governor, we would not rest until we had placed that notice in the proper hands to secure his release. We wouldn't let anything get in our way to hinder us.

Rescuing souls requires hard, faithful work. Jude said some souls must be saved by "pulling them out of the fire" (Jude 1:23). However, one must bear the heat and discomfort of the fire in order to do it. To save those who are being drowned, we must take the risk and plunge into the water ourselves.

What we need, as Christians, is the same loyal spirit that was manifested by a regiment in the English army when they were preparing to attack the stronghold of the enemy. The general explained that storming the fortification would be extremely dangerous, and many would not survive. Then he asked all who would be willing to volunteer for the service to take one step forward. Instantly, every soldier advanced one step. If men fighting for an earthly kingdom and glory could do that, shouldn't we, who are engaged in the closing struggle against the powers of darkness, be as brave also?

Chapter Six – Too Late!

Too late! There are no more melancholy words than these in the entire English language. As fast as he can go, the messenger conveys the news to a son that his father is in the grip of death. Upon receiving the news, the son runs home as fast as he can, only to learn that his father has already breathed his last breath. He is too late.

A skillful doctor is called to hurry to the bedside of a dying man in hopes of saving him. He rushes to the room, but when he arrives, the death damp has gathered, and as he looks in sadness on his patient, in subdued tones, he informs the sorrowing friends and family that he is too late.

An anxious crowd gathers around a building wrapped in flames while the victims trapped inside are trying to escape. The fire engines rush to the spot, and everything possible is done to extinguish the flames, but they are not fast enough. The building is soon consumed, and the inmates perish because their help arrived too late.

In the distance, a vessel is smashing against the rocks, and the waves are quickly tearing the great ship to pieces. The terror-stricken passengers imploringly plead for help. From the shore, the rescue team sees her distress and makes their way out to sea in the teeth of the storm, only to reach the doomed vessel just as she sinks before their eyes. They were too late to save the precious cargo of lives.

As heart-rending as these scenes are, they are not as sad as the sight of a sinner gone down in sin, lost forever, with all efforts to reach him forever too late! Today is indeed the day of salvation. The lost souls who may still be reached today could be out of our reach tomorrow.

All around us, people are making this sad and irretrievable mistake of total indifference concerning the life to come. Sin fascinates them. Friends and worldly companions urge them on in the pleasures of the world, but out of the blue, the cold hand of death sweeps over them. Finally, their sun sets in darkness, as in the following story, which took place in the 1800s.

"A young lady in New York attended a revival meeting with her parents. A godly aunt became greatly troubled over the condition of the young lady, who was unconverted. As the appeal was made at the end of the meeting, she earnestly began to plead with her to seek God this night, but the girl refused. After the meeting, she started home with her parents, but a short way from the church, the horses became frightened and overthrew the sleigh. The young lady was violently thrown against a telephone pole and instantly killed." She had put off seeking God, and now it was too late.

I had an experience once while traveling, which I hope to never forget. It taught me what a person can do to help those in need if they just have their eyes opened. It also showed me how easy it is to miss opportunities, only to awaken too late to the fact that there was someone right beside us in need of help and sympathy. The incident occurred as I was riding from Buffalo to Washington. Soon after leaving the train station, I noticed a nicely dressed gentleman, somewhat gray on top, sitting just across the aisle from me. If I recall correctly, he had four little children with him. The fact that he had so many small children with him got my attention, and I thought that the man was a bit careless to go on such a long journey alone, with so many children.

As we rode on, hour after hour, the children became restless, and two of the little girls came to my seat, looking up at me as if they wanted to talk to me, but I didn't have time to spend with them. I was a preacher, and I had to do some reading to prepare for my lectures. I wasn't in the mood to be bothered by children, so I continued reading my books, with no concern for the children, or interest in the man's situation.

Finally, as we were nearing Baltimore, I was getting tired of reading, and being curious where this man was going, I started to talk to him. He seemed like he was glad to have someone to talk to. In our conversation, I mentioned his children and how nice it would have been if their mother could have been with them for such a long trip. Looking up, he said, "Oh, their mother is along. She is riding in the baggage car."

I learned more in that instant than I learned all day from my books. I can't even remember what I was reading now, but I have never forgotten what that man said; "Riding in the baggage car." I knew then why he was alone with his children. In a few short words, he told me how his home had been broken up by death and of the sorrow in his heart. He said that he was taking his wife back to the place where, when a young man, he had won her for his wife, to lay her to rest in the family burial ground. Then I saw a tear steal down his cheek, and one sweet little girl said, "Papa, why are you crying?"

I felt like weeping too and thought that if I was only back at the beginning of the journey, I could have helped him take care of his motherless children. Soon we reached Baltimore, and he got off the train with his little ones. I got off to see where he went. I saw the pine box containing the wife and mother of his children shoved out of the baggage car and onto a cart. Then I watched him as he, with the four little children, followed the remains around to the other side of the train.

I have never seen that man since. I lost my chance to help him. I was too late. But I learned a lesson that day that I have always tried to remember, and I have endeavored to be more watchful for people in need of help.

Probation's hour is fast closing. Some will delay and will finally exclaim, "The harvest is past, the summer is ended, and we are not saved" (Jer. 8:20). Life is uncertain, and it will soon be too late to work for the lost. As Christians, we should be diligent in our efforts to bring the light of the gospel to those who are unsaved. If we delay, we may find that the great opportunity of a lifetime is past.

You are a Christian, but perhaps your neighbor is not. Today he is within your reach. An opportunity to share the gospel with him presents itself. Perhaps some sorrow has come into his life, and he longs for sympathy. His heart is tender. Today your friend is near you. For years you have had so many sweet memories together. Now his heart is ripe to hear the gospel. Today your child is with you. His heart is tender, and he is ready to yield to the impulses of the Holy Spirit. Will you tell him?

Today is the day of salvation. Life is uncertain. Who knows what a day may bring. Speak now. Don't remain silent any longer. Point those without hope to Jesus today, because tomorrow may be too late. Now is your chance. Don't miss it, because soon this great opportunity will be gone, and gone forever.

It is good to reflect on our lives as Christians. Think of our families, friends, and neighbors. Have we done all we can for their salvation? Have we pleaded with them to give their hearts to God before it is too late? In our prayer closet, have our eyes run with tears for the lost around us? People die every day. Every hour people are drifting out of our reach, but there are still people around us crying in their hearts for God to send someone to rescue them. There is still time.

What are your plans for the future? Will you keep living the same as you have always lived, or will you take hold of God with a renewed vigor, pleading for strength and power to help rescue those within your reach before they are gone forever? I pray you will seek God to make a change today.

FREE BIBLE STUDIES

MAKE PRAYER REQUESTS

WATCH VIDEOS ONLINE

READ AND DOWNLOAD BOOKS AND TRACTS

PURCHASE MATERIALS AND GET INVOLVED!

www.hopetracts.com